HUNTING Coloring Book

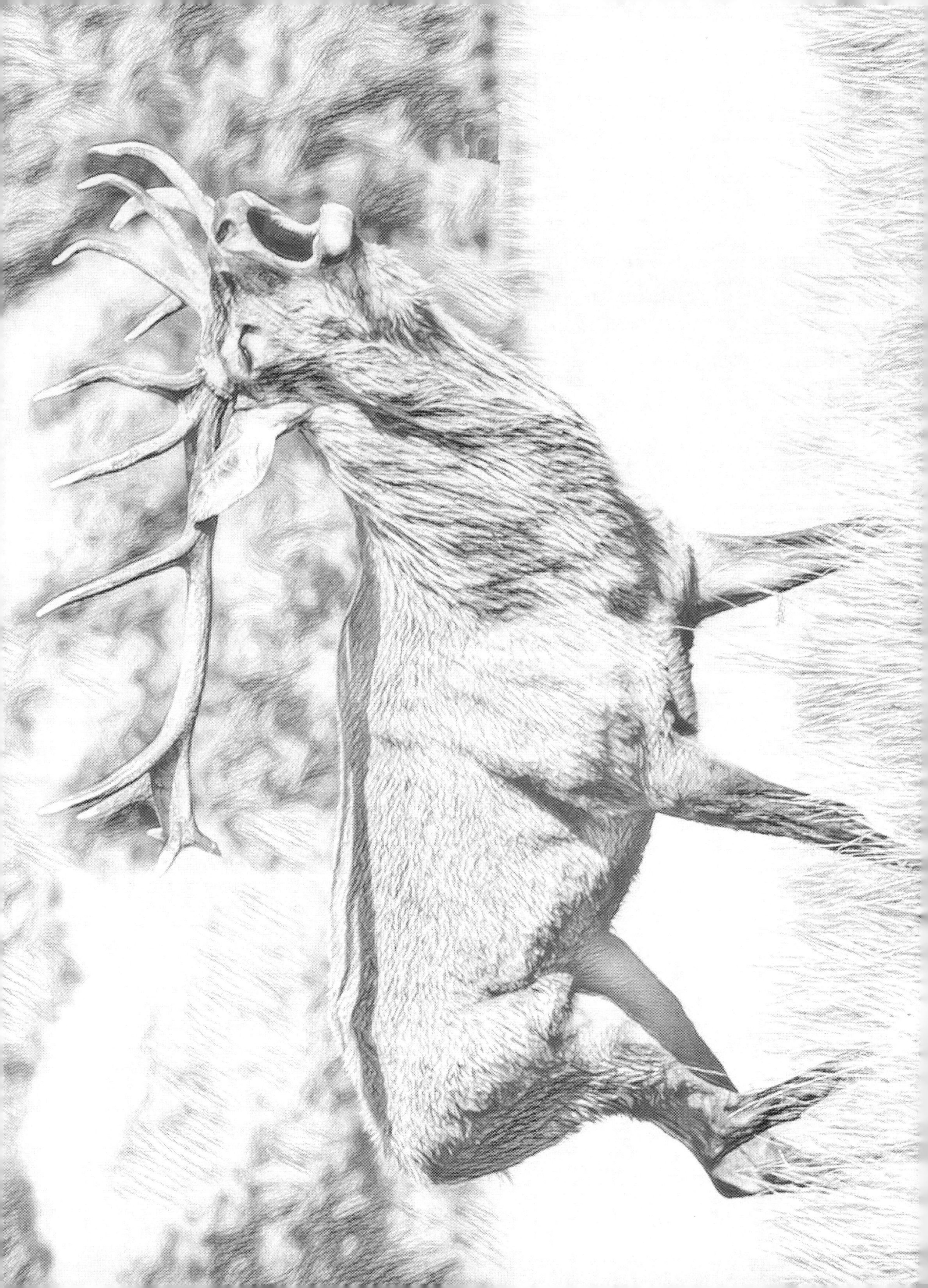

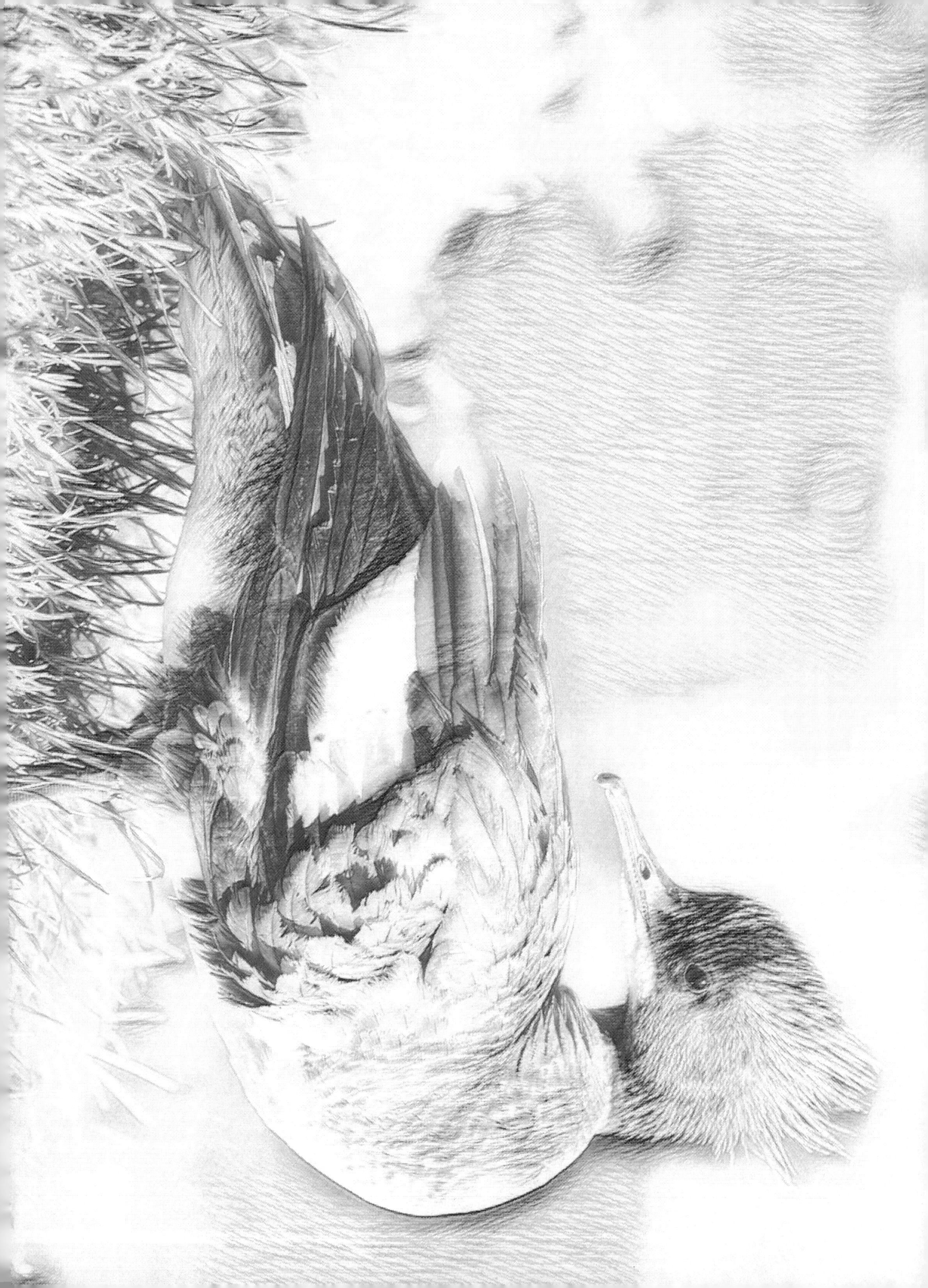

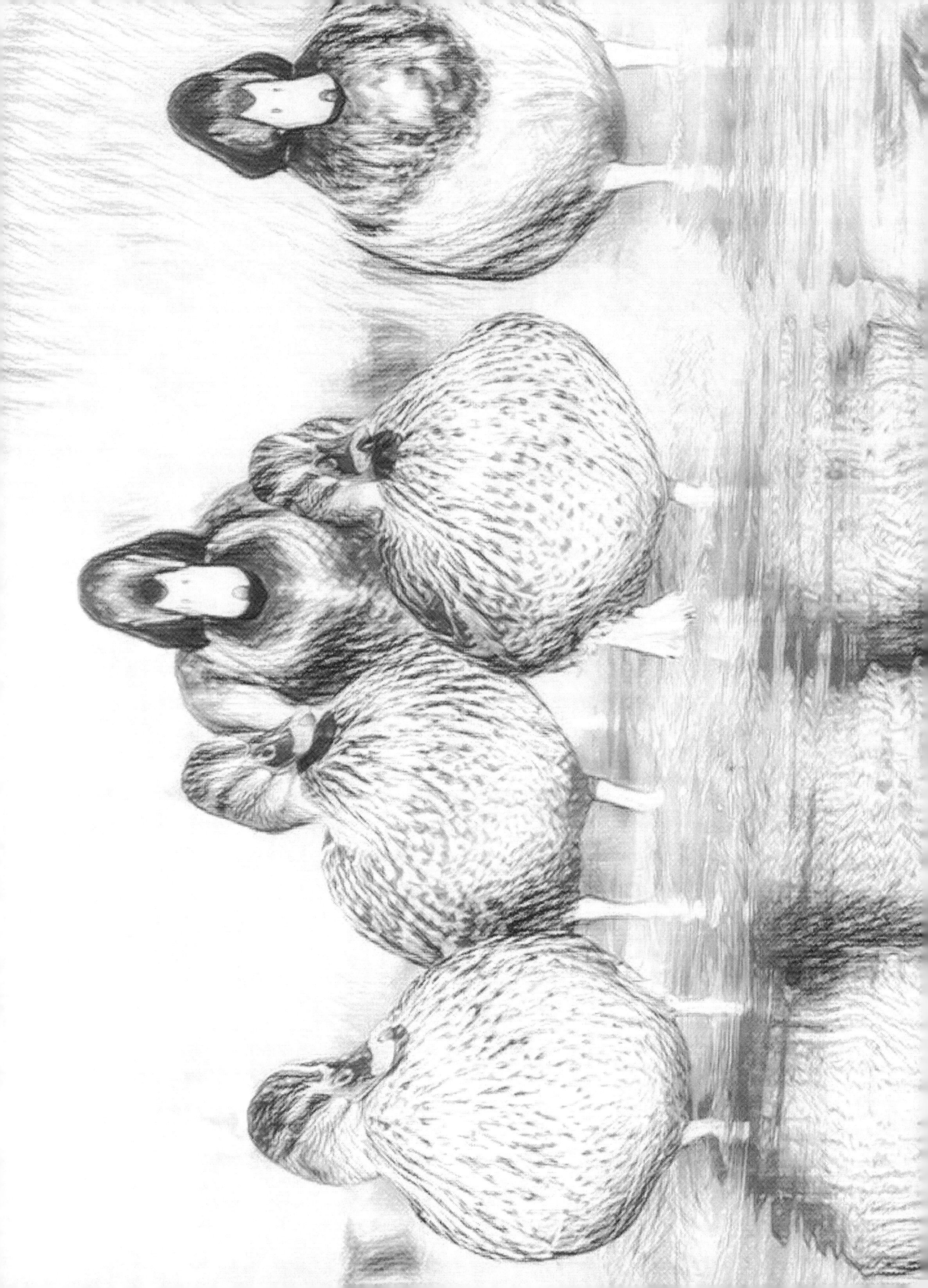

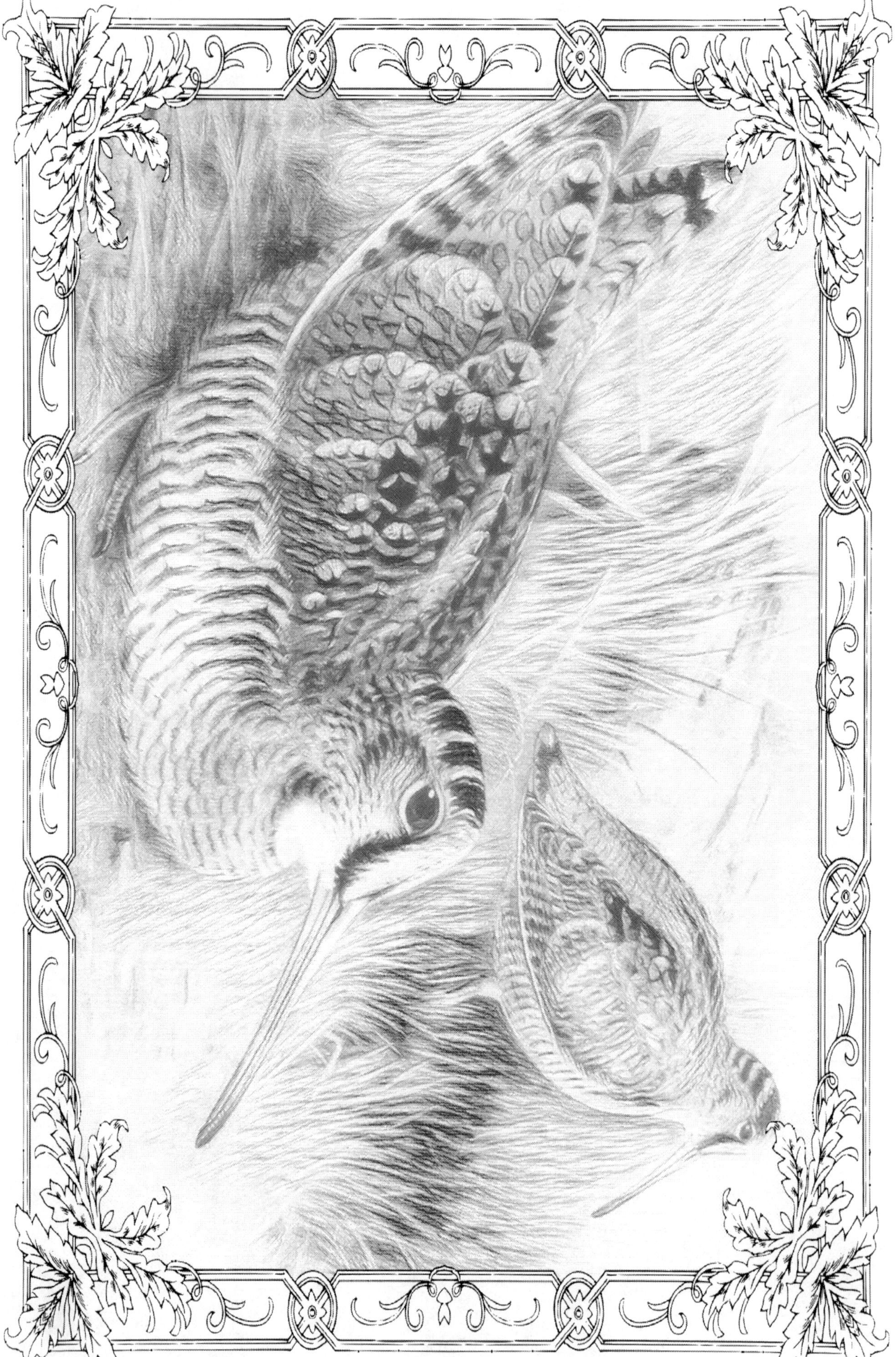

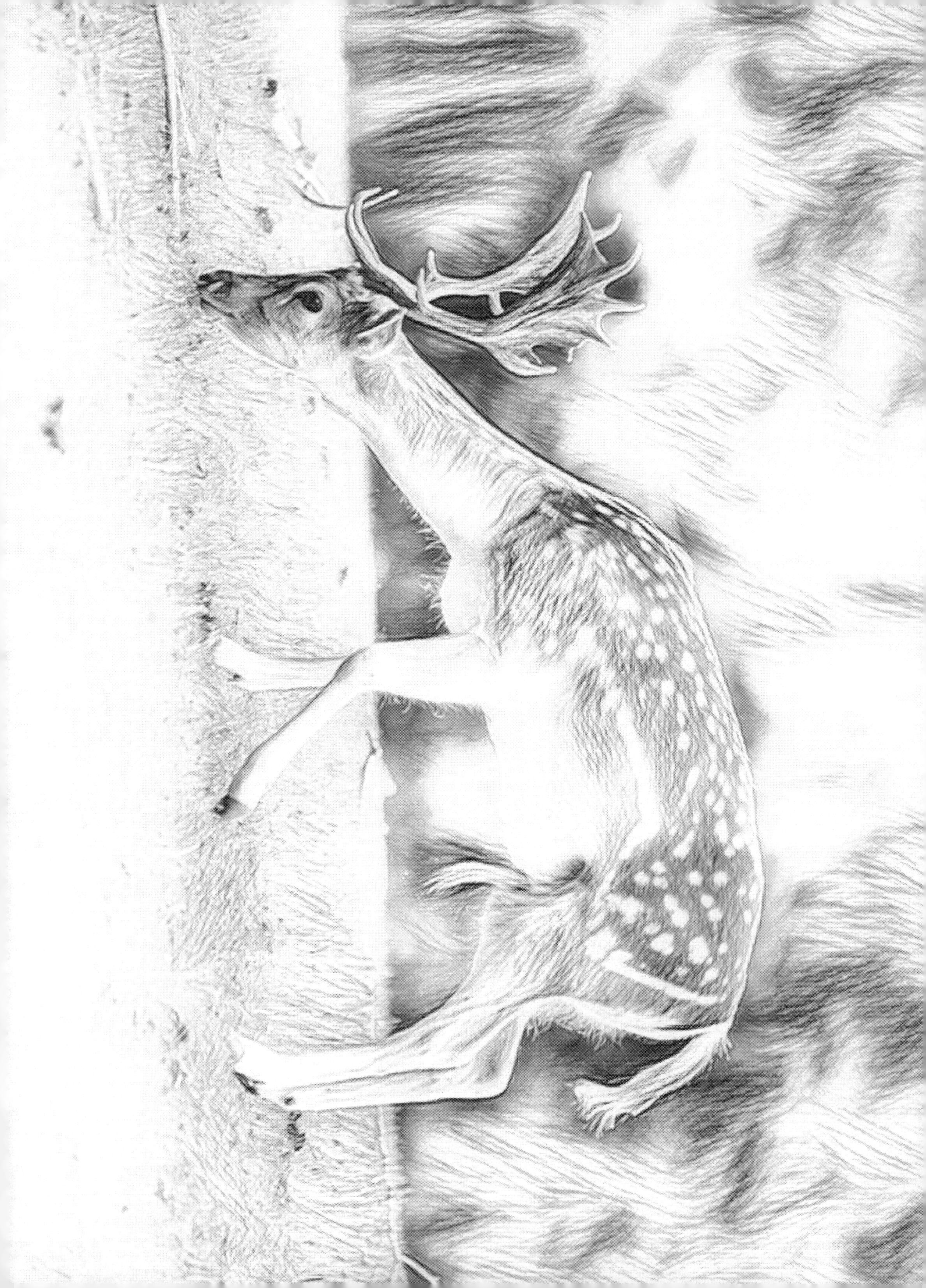

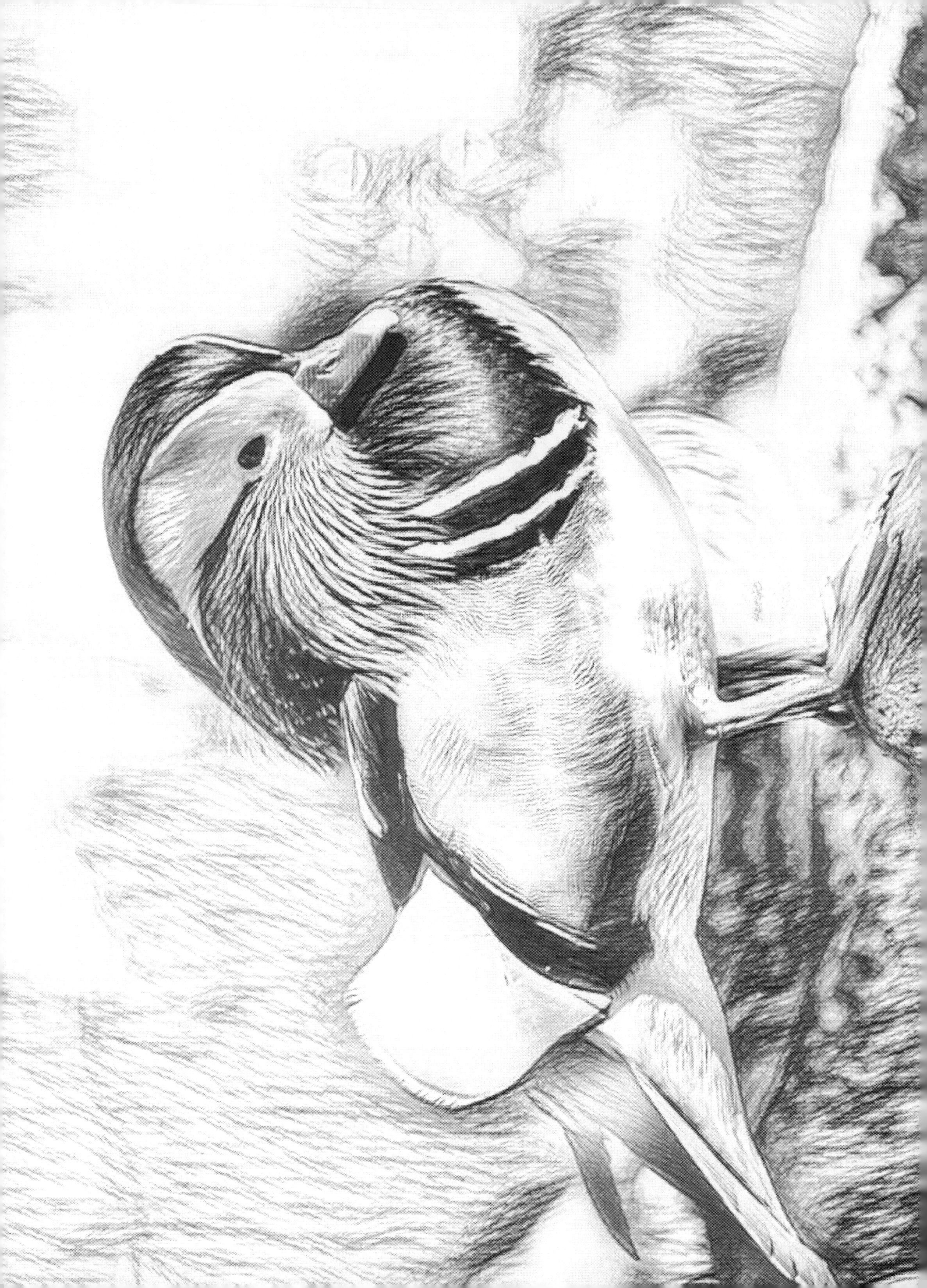

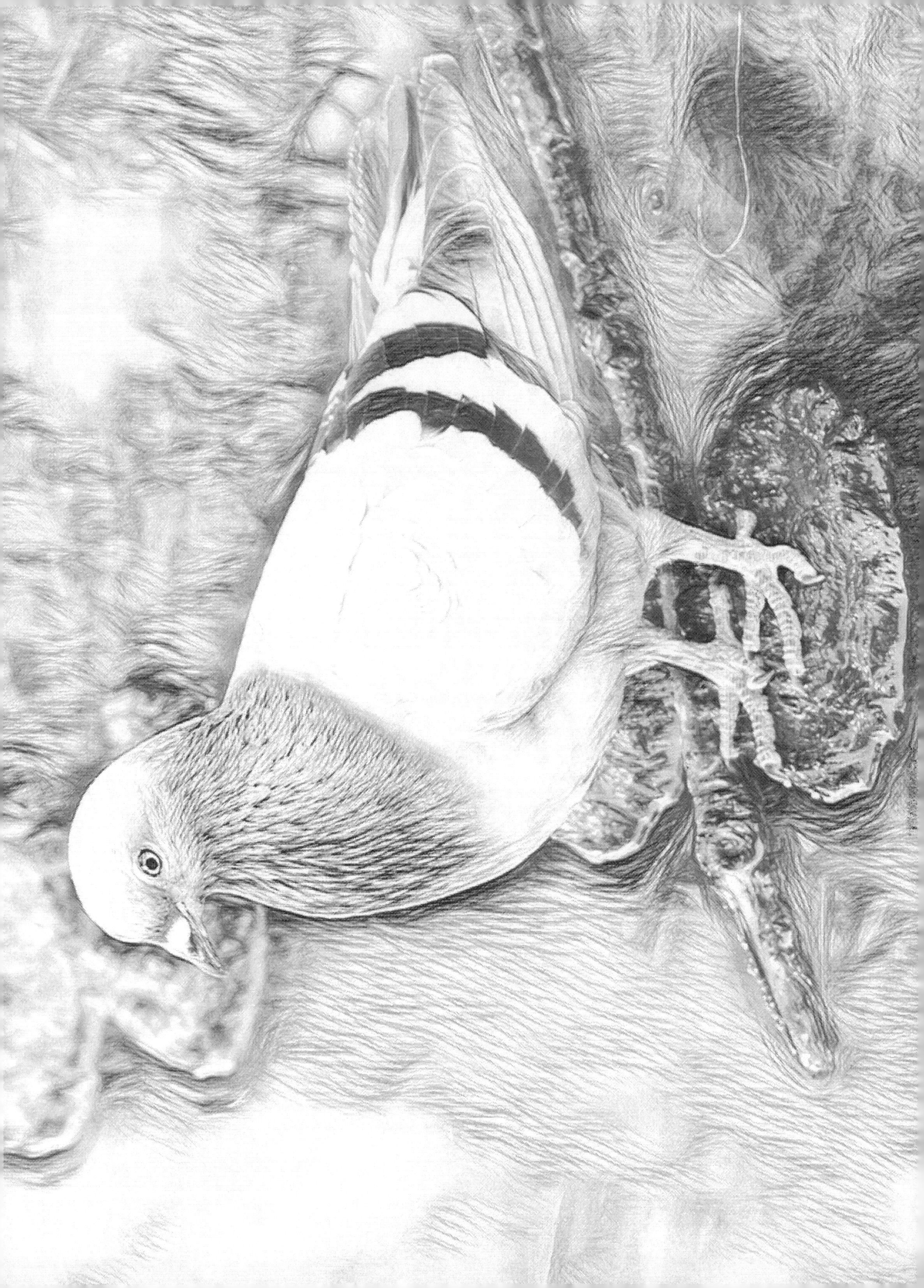

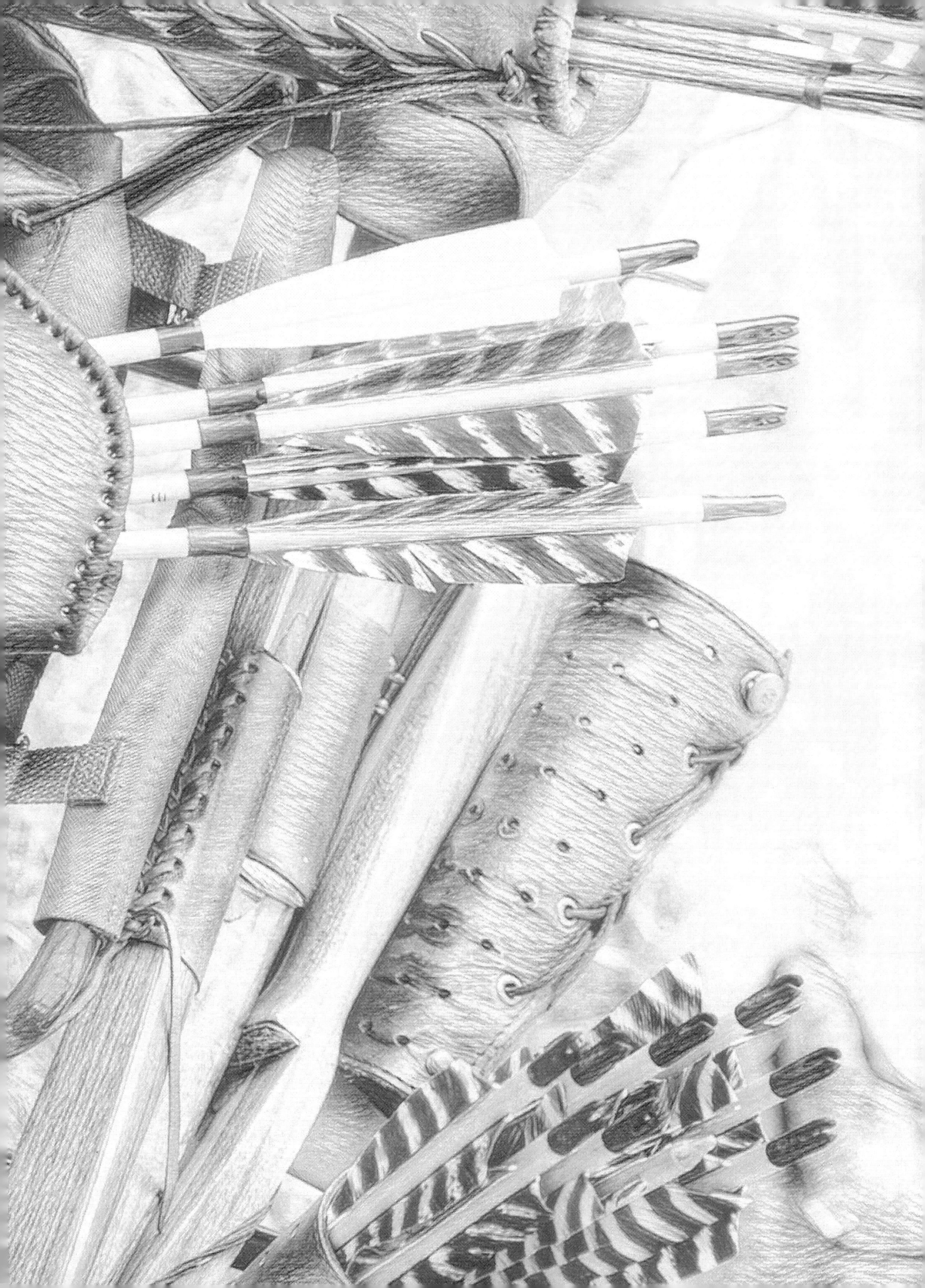

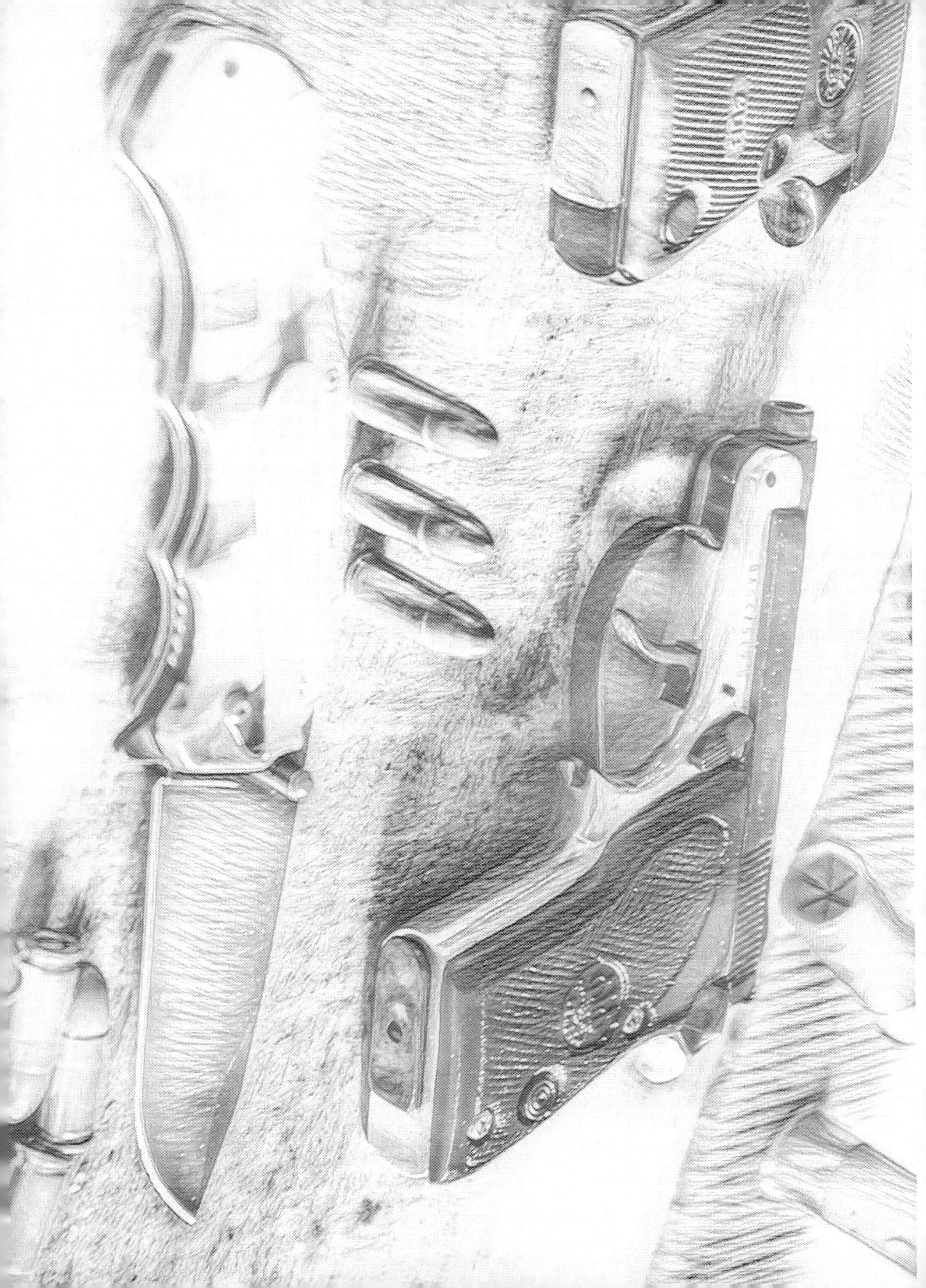

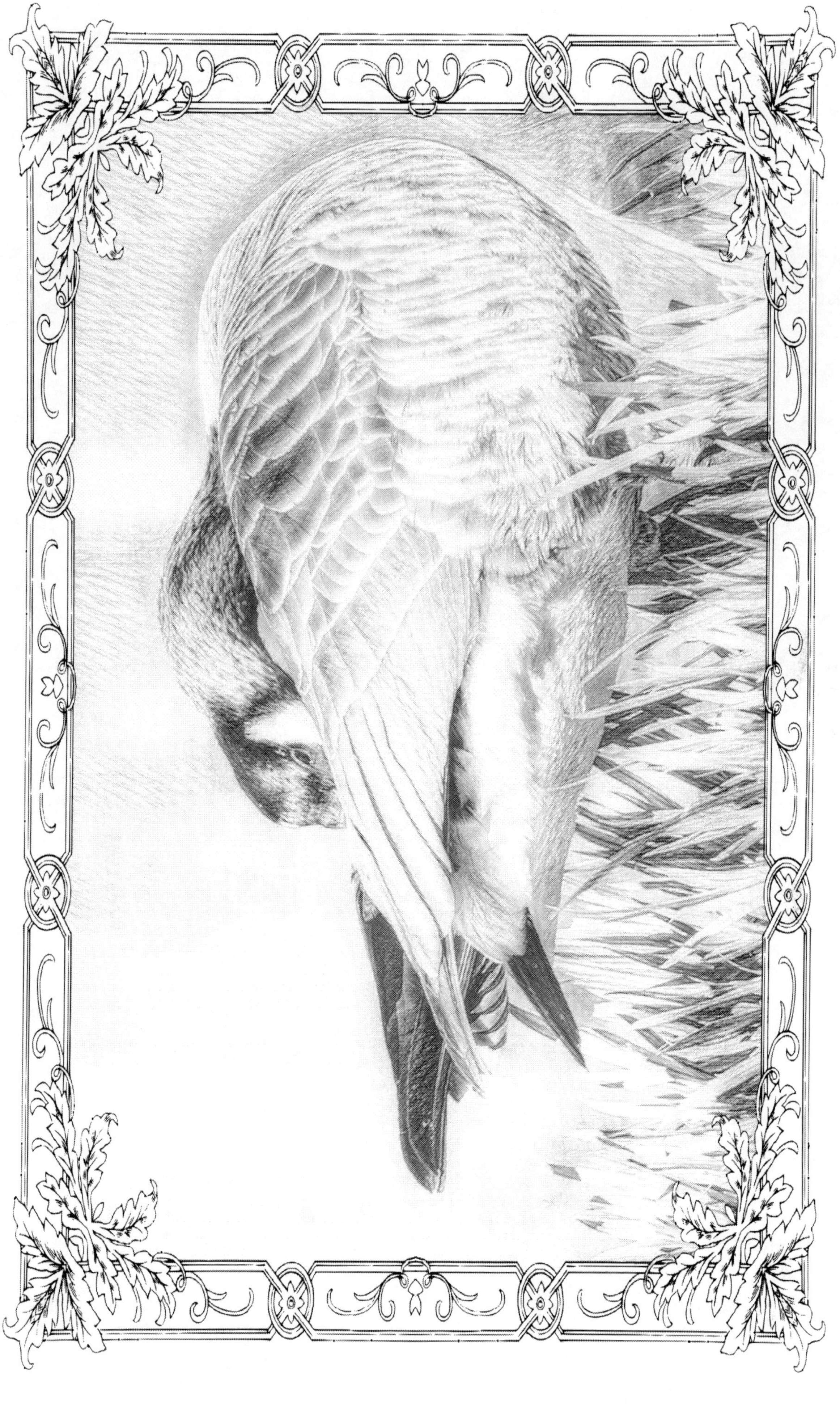

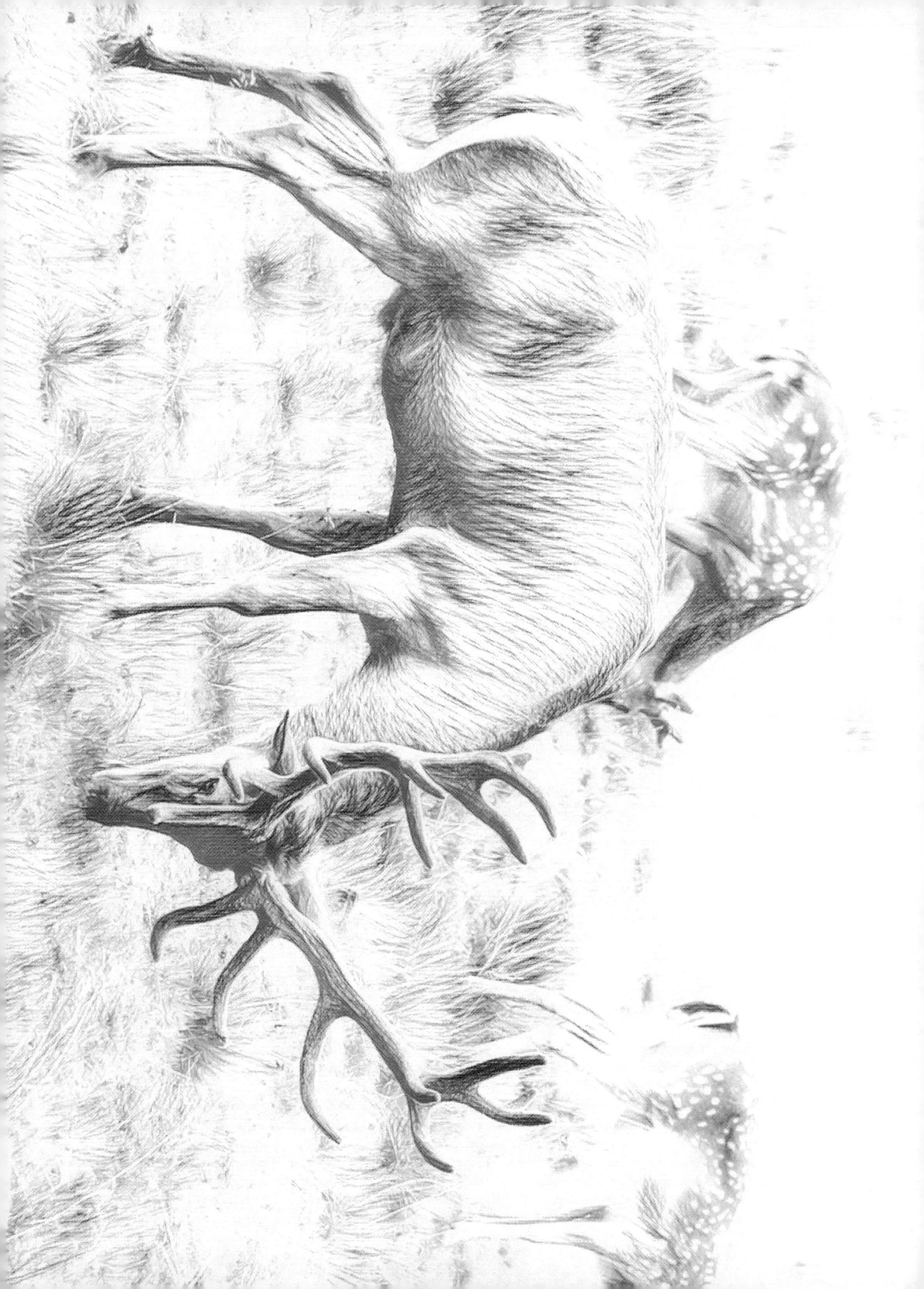

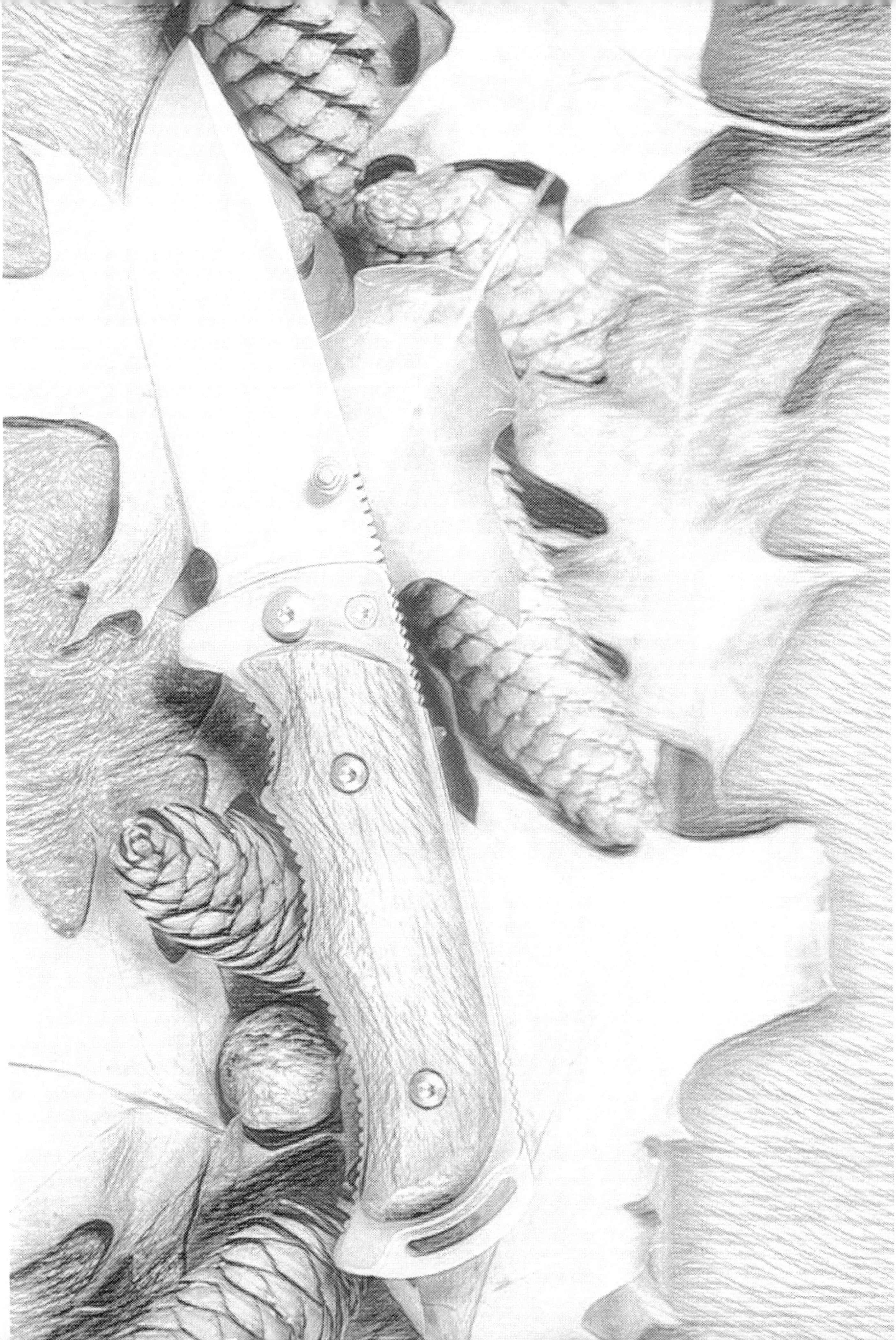

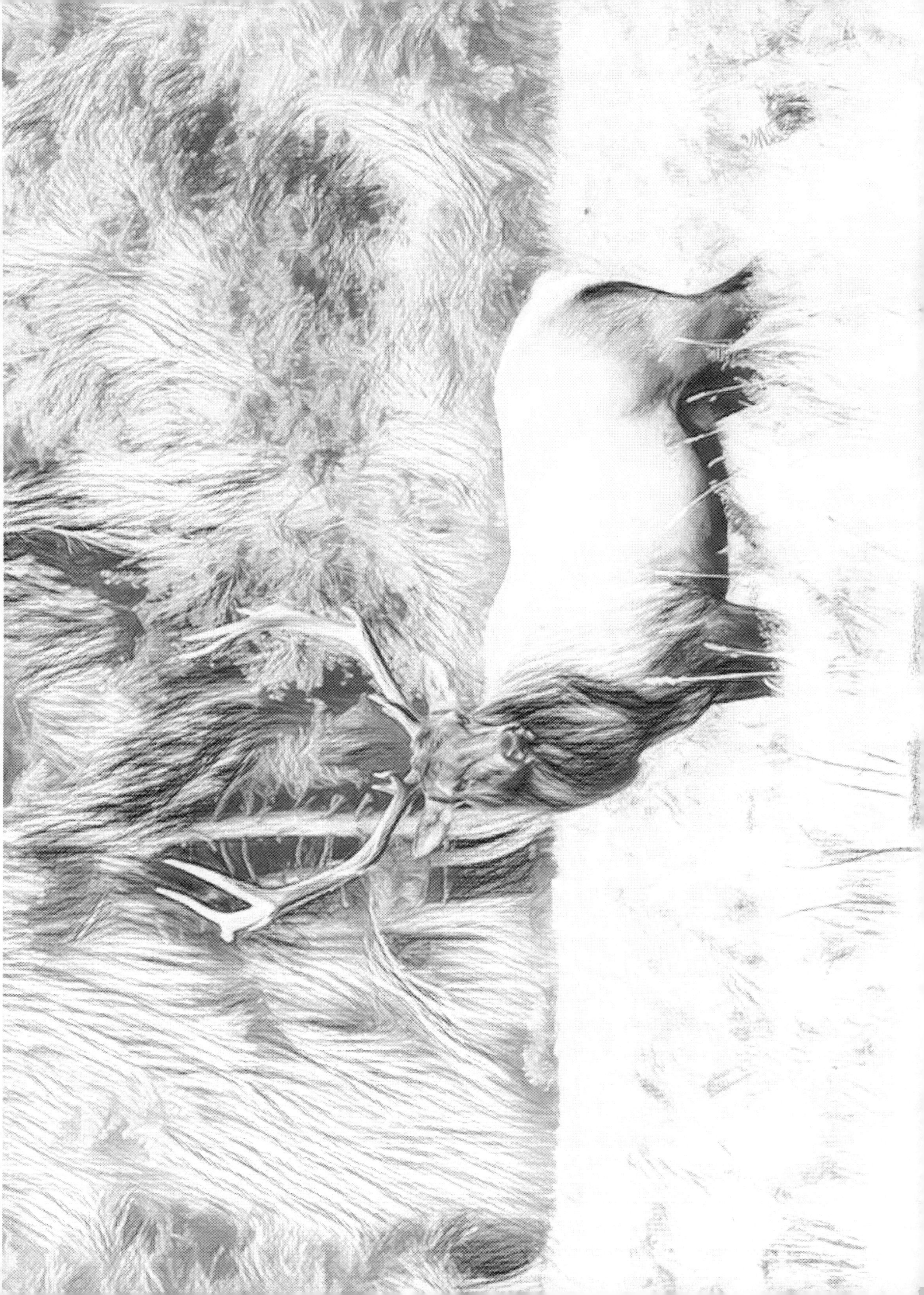

Made in United States
Troutdale, OR
10/02/2023

13345232R00046